Maurice Pledger

Bobby Bear's
STICKER BOOK

Written by A.J. Wood

In the Field and Forest

Silver Dolphin

Published in the United States by

Silver Dolphin Books

An imprint of the Advantage Publishers Group

5880 Oberlin Drive, San Diego, CA 92121-4794

www.advantagebooksonline.com

Written by A.J. Wood. Concept by Sydney Stanley

Designed by Mike Jolley

ISBN 1-57145-384-9

Printed in Italy by STIGE

4 5   01 02 03

How to use this book

This colorful and fun sticker book is a gentle introduction to some of the wonderful wildlife inhabiting Bobby Bear's world. You'll meet such familiar friends as Billy Bunny, Morris Mouse, Olivia Owl, and Winnie Wolf in this book that features 72 pages of activities and stories and 24 pages of reusable stickers.

Have fun as you:

● Fill in the picture gallery as you meet each of Bobby Bear's friends

● Find bug and animal stickers to match the outlines provided

● Complete scenes using story clues

● Match animals to their habitats

● Make up your own stories and create imaginative pictures to illustrate them

See page 72 for some information about how to pick the right stickers for each activity page. And remember, after you finish the activities you can reuse the 150 stickers again and again to decorate whatever you want.

Over the hills and far away is a special forest where all of the animals talk and are good friends. All sorts of creatures live there. There's Winnie Wolf, Billy Bunny, Morris Mouse, and Olivia Owl.

One of the friendliest animals is Bobby Bear, a little black bear cub. Bobby loves to explore. He's always looking for some honey to eat, but he finds lots of other interesting things as well. Why don't you join him and see what exciting discoveries you can make? Along the way you'll meet lots of Bobby's friends.

Bobby's friends

Bobby Bear has lots of animal friends. They like to go exploring in the field and forest, too. Bobby's best friend is Billy Bunny, whom you'll meet later.

Use stickers from sheet 1 to fill in Bobby Bear's photo album friends. Which animal would you like as your best friend?

Winnie Wolf

Olivia Owl

Billy Bunny

Morris Mouse

Willy Weasel

B obby Bear is always on the lookout for bees! He hopes that they will lead him to some honey! But bees aren't the only insects that he has discovered in the forest. Everywhere he looks there are other tiny creatures going about their business.

Use the stickers from sheet 1 to fill in the spaces
to show some other creatures that Bobby found.

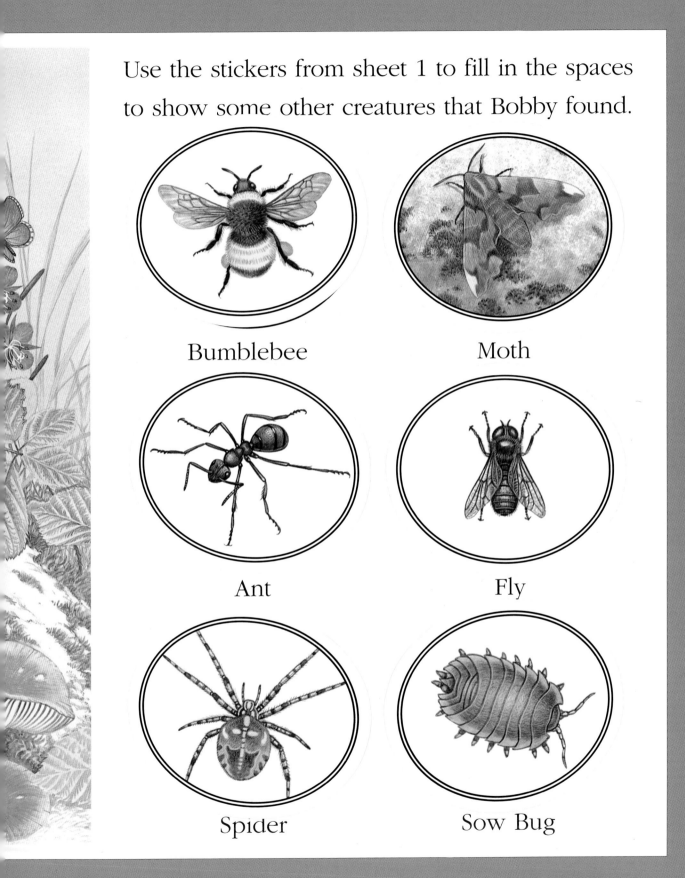

Bumblebee

Moth

Ant

Fly

Spider

Sow Bug

Find five beetles

Apart from bees, Bobby Bear's favorite little creatures are the beetles. He loves their bright colors and different shapes. Can you find five colorful beetles on sticker sheet 2 that match the ones below?

Furry friends

Bobby Bear has lovely black fur. There are lots of other furry animals in the forest, too. Here is Bobby's friend Cheeky Chipmunk. He has one of the softest, furriest tails of all. Use the stickers from sheet 2 to fill in the pictures of five other furry forest friends.

Sally Squirrel

Freddy Fox

Molly Mouse

Ricky Raccoon

Beth Badger

W ho do you think Bobby and his friends Cheeky Chipmunk, Ricky Raccoon, and Olivia Owl have discovered down at the old log? Use your stickers to add Curly Quail, Jenny Wren, a snail, and two colorful butterflies to the picture.

Look at the pictures in the ovals and find the stickers on sheet 2 that match.

Collecting leaves

Do you ever collect leaves in the forest? When Fall comes and the leaves fall to the ground, you can find leaves in all sorts of different shapes and colors. Jilly Jay has used some to make her nest. See if you can find some more leaves for her by looking on sheet 3 for four different leaf stickers that match the ones below.

B

obby Bear has been looking everywhere in the forest for his friends, Olivia Owl and Winnie Wolf. Cheeky Chipmunk thinks they might be hiding down by the old pine tree.

Help Bobby by using the stickers on sheet 3 to add Olivia and Winnie to the picture.

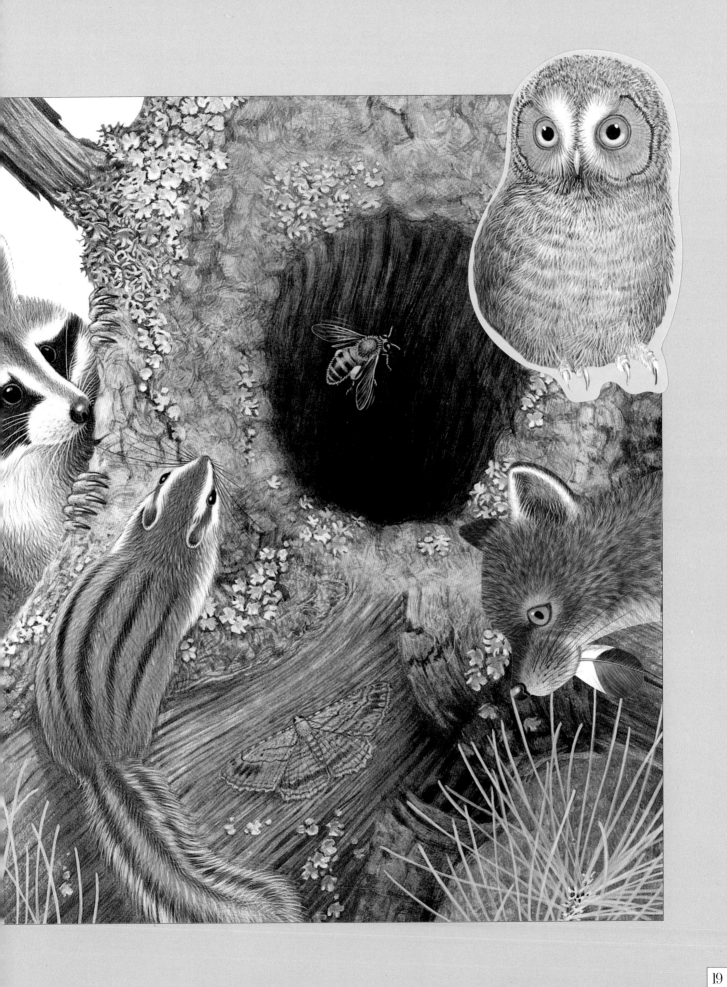

Use the stickers on sheet 6 to make a picture of the things that Bobby finds down at the old log.

20

Find five feathers

Winnie, the little gray wolf cub, likes exploring in the forest, too, especially when she discovers a new feather for her collection. Can you help her by finding five different feathers on sticker sheet 3 to match the ones shown here?

One day Winnie Wolf was out hunting feathers when she found some strange plants growing on the forest floor.

"What are these?" she asked Lance Lizard. Lanc told her that they were mushrooms. Use the stickers on sheets 3 and 4 to fill in the spaces with all of the things that Winnie discovered or her trip through the forest.

Acorns

Pine Cone

Mushrooms

Berries

Lance says: "Remember, never pick mushrooms, berries, or nuts. And never, ever put them in your mouth. Some of them can make you very sick."

Guess who Winnie Wolf and Lance Lizard meet on their journey through the forest? Why, it's Olivia Owl. Now they are all friends. Use the sticker on sheet 4 to put her in the picture.

Find these three things to add to the picture—a
yellow slug, a flying beetle, and Molly, the little
wood mouse.

Find five moths

Olivia Owl explores the forest when the sun goes down! She finds all sorts of different creatures that only come out once it starts to get dark. She meets bats and badgers, mice, and her favorite of all, the moths.

Find the stickers on sheet 4 that match five of Olivia's favorite moths.

Wings in the wood

Look! Olivia has found another moth. And that's not all—Goldy Goldcrest is playing hide-and-seek behind the trees with five of Olivia's feathered friends. Use the stickers on sheets 4 and 5 to fill in the pictures of Olivia's bird buddies.

Sandra
Sparrow

Winston
Woodpecker

Henry
Hummingbird

enny
Wren

Betty
Bluetit

What else has Olivia discovered on the forest floor? Look carefully at the picture. Is there a stripy snail somewhere? Can you see a spotty ladybug hiding? How many feathers has Olivia left behind?

Use the stickers on sheet 5 to add four more things to the picture—a bumblebee, a flower, another snail, and a beautiful moth.

Who lives here?

Cheeky Chipmunk is visiting Freddy Fox in his den at the bottom of the old oak tree. Use the sticker on sheet 5 to add Freddy to the picture. Now put these other animals back in their homes—a spider in its web, a bird in its nest, and a bee in its hive.

Can you guess who lives in this hole in the tree trunk? Why, Olivia Owl of course!

Use the stickers on sheet 6 to make up your own picture of animals in the branches of this tree.

36

A t the edge of Bobby Bear's forest is the meadow where his friends Morris Mouse and Willy Weasel live. It is also where he goes to play with his very best friend, Billy Bunny. Use the stickers on sheet 5 to add Billy, Morris, and Willy to the scene.

Who else can
you see in the
picture?

Find five butterflies

Billy Bunny loves to look for butterflies in the meadow. There are so many different kinds! So far he has found four beautiful butterflies. Can you use the stickers on sheet 7 to find five more to match the ones below?

Changing shape

Billy thinks that butterflies are extra special creatures because they change shape as they grow. When butterflies are babies they don't look like butterflies at all! Follow the numbers to see how a butterfly grows up.

7

Then find a beautiful butterfly sticker on sheet 7 to put in the space above.

6

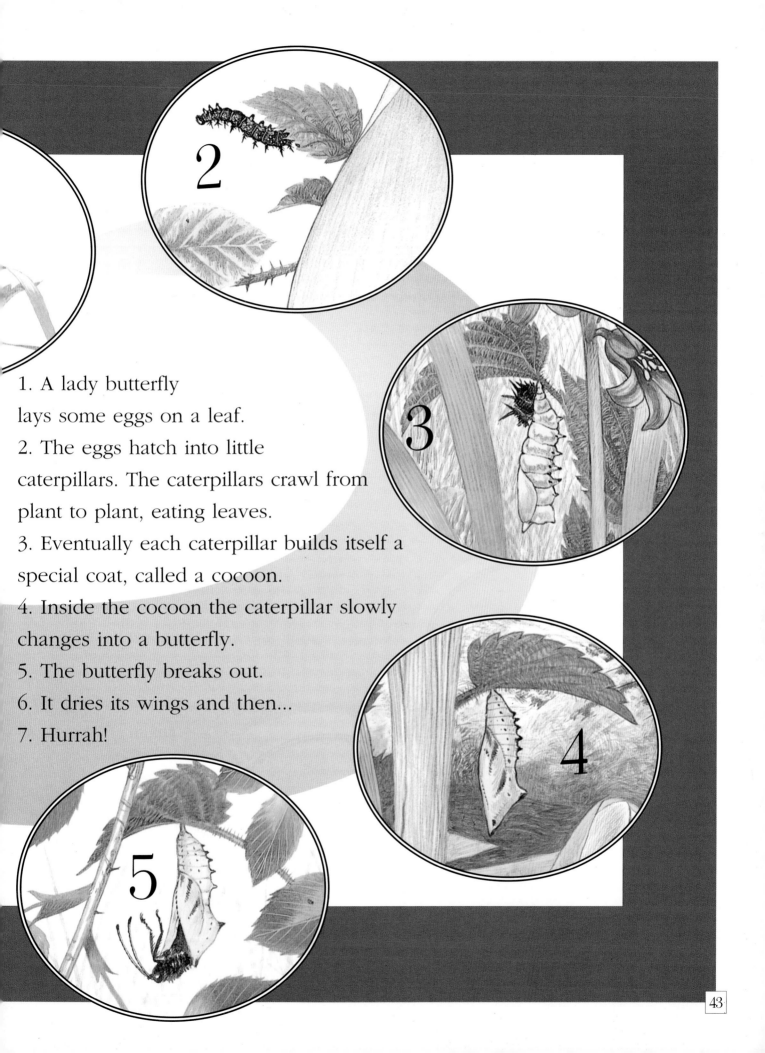

1. A lady butterfly
lays some eggs on a leaf.
2. The eggs hatch into little
caterpillars. The caterpillars crawl from
plant to plant, eating leaves.
3. Eventually each caterpillar builds itself a
special coat, called a cocoon.
4. Inside the cocoon the caterpillar slowly
changes into a butterfly.
5. The butterfly breaks out.
6. It dries its wings and then...
7. Hurrah!

Field friends

When Billy Bunny isn't busy playing with his friend Bobby Bear he likes to go exploring in the bushes that run along the edge of the field. Lots of small creatures live there. Fill in the spaces with their pictures using stickers from sheet 7.

Hoppy Frog

Grasshoppers

Vinnie Vole

Sammy Skunk

Tommy Toad   Snail

Can you see what Billy has discovered today on his walk through the field? He has found a beautiful ladybug hiding among the leaves. Can you see someone else who's hiding there, too? Yes, it's Molly Mouse!

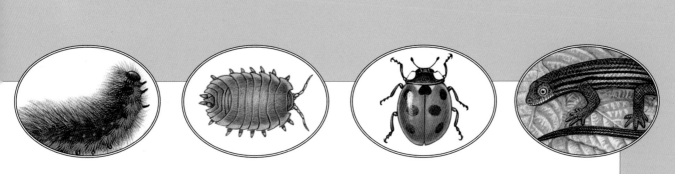

Now complete the picture by adding stickers from sheet 7 of four other things for Billy to find—Lance Lizard, a caterpillar, a sow bug, and another ladybug.

Meadow flowers

Look! Billy has found some lovely yellow flowers growing in the meadow. They are called primroses. Use the stickers from sheet 8 to fill in the ovals with some other colorful flowers that Billy has discovered.

Bluebell

Wild Rose

Forget-Me-Not

Violet

Foxglove

Make your own picture of the field
by adding stickers from sheet 12 to this scene.

50

Here's Billy Bunny sitting down for a rest at the edge of the meadow. He's had such a busy morning exploring that he's tired himself out! He's been looking everywhere for his friend Morris the little harvest mouse. Can you help him by adding a sticker of Morris from sheet 8 to the picture?

As well as Morris Mouse, add stickers of a butterfly, some grasshoppers, and another bluebell to the scene. What other creatures can you see?

Find five caterpillars

Morris Mouse is always
finding caterpillars
in his field.

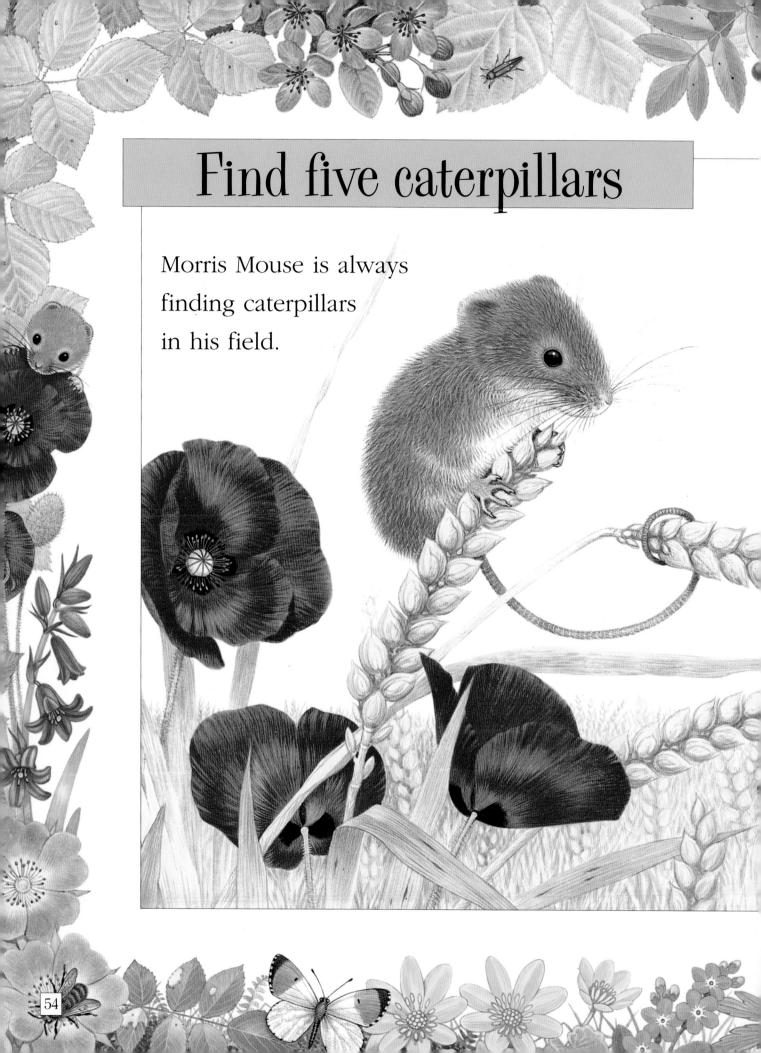

They come in all sorts of colors and shapes. Today he is making a collection of caterpillars to show to his friends. Would you like to help him? Use the stickers from sheet 8 to find five different caterpillars to match the ones below.

Footprints in the field

Bobby Bear and his friends have very differently shaped feet. Sometimes they leave their footprints in the mud at the edge of the field. Can you guess who these six sets of footprints belong to? Fill in the ovals by matching the footprint shapes with the correct animal from sheet 9.

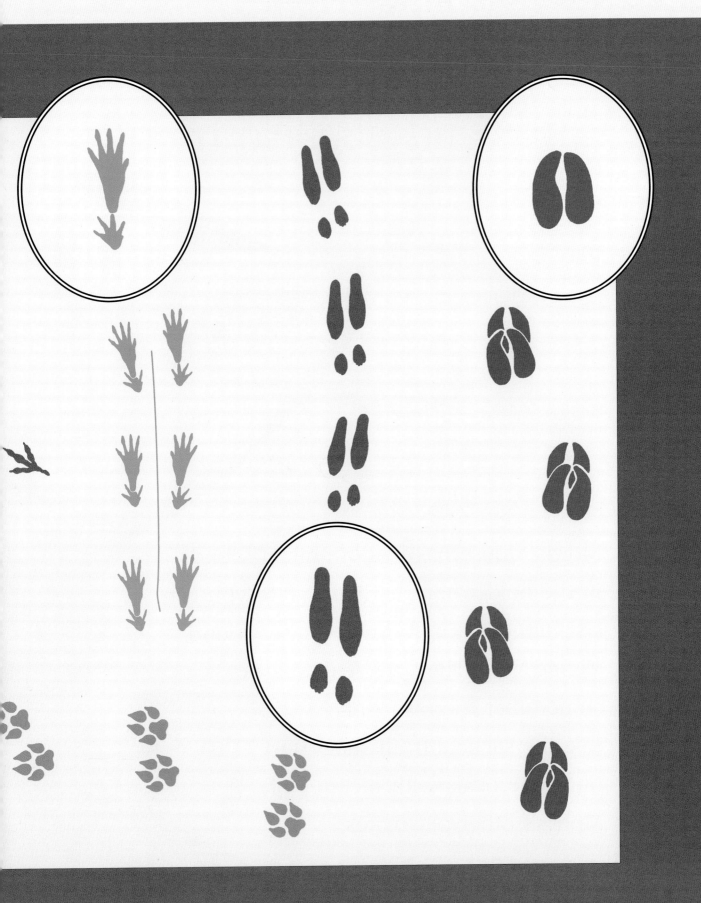

Morris and his field friends

Morris Mouse has lots of animal friends in the field where he lives. Here you can see him climbing a tree with his friend Vinnie Vole. They are searching for some other friends to play with. Use the stickers from sheet 9 to fill in the ovals with pictures of Morris's other playmates.

Dilly Dormouse

Max Mole

Swifty Swallow

Curly Quail

Harriet Hare

Danny Deer

Who lives here?

Morris Mouse lives in a cozy nest right in the middle of his field. He made it all by himself from leaves and grass woven into a big ball. You can see three other animal homes here. Use the stickers from sheet 10 to put the right animal back in its home and don't forget to add Morris to the space below.

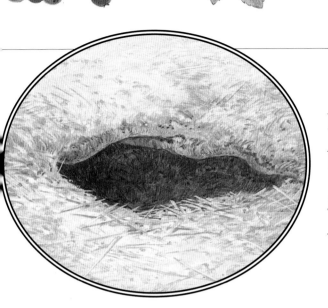

Billy Bunny lives in a big burrow underneath the ground. It is called a warren.

Harriet Hare spends nearly all her time running around the field. But when her babies are born she makes a special dip in the grass for them to hide in. It is called a form.

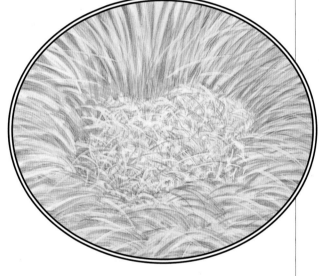

Jenny Wren makes a special nest in which to lay her eggs. She hides it deep in the bush.

Field flowers

In the summer Morris Mouse often finds beautiful flowers growing in his field. Today he has discovered a big white flower that looks just like a trumpet. Use the stickers from sheet 10 to fill in the pictures of some other lovely flowers that Morris might find.

Thistle

Poppy

Buttercup

Daisy

ook! Morris has found some fallen apples at the edge of the field. He thinks that they will make a fine feast for him and his friend Willy Weasel, but the trouble is he can't find Willy anywhere. Can you help him by using a sticker from sheet 10 to add Willy to the picture?

Now add some of Morris's other friends to the scene. Vinnie Vole, a moth, and two butterflies have all come to join the feast as well.

Find five berries

Willy Weasel loves to collect berries in the autumn. Can you help him by finding five different berries from sheet 11 to match the shapes shown here. And remember, never eat berries yourself when you're out exploring the countryside. Some of them can make you very sick.

All sorts of animals have gathered down at the old stump. Can you see Willy Weasel and Morris Mouse? Can you see Dilly Dormouse and Sally Squirrel? Who else can you see? Use the stickers from sheet 11 to add four more animals to the picture—Hoppy Frog, Jenny Wren, Billy Bunny, and Bobby Bear.

Use the stickers from sheet 12 to make up your own picture of the field where Morris Mouse lives.

How to use your stickers

Look for the page numbers on the sticker sheets. They will help you find the right stickers for the different activities in this book.

Peel each sticker carefully from its backing sheet and stick it in the right place in the book. The stickers on sheets 6 and 12 contain lots and lots of stickers for you to make up your own pictures. You can use them with the big scenes in the book. Or you could draw your own picture of the special place where Bobby Bear lives with all his animal friends and stick them on that!